LB2805
G6

Goldstein, W.

Supervision made simple.

DATE DUE			
14 2005			

PRAIRIE STATE COLLEGE

CHICAGO HEIGHTS, ILL.

This fastback is sponsored by the Valdosta State College Chapter (Georgia) of Phi Delta Kappa, which made a generous contribution toward publication costs.

Table of Contents

Will Real Evaluation Please Stand Up 7

Of Managerial Myths and Fairy Tales 9

Seeing What Should Be Seen: Quality in the Classroom 13

Checklists vs. Narratives: Which to Use, How, and When ... 20

Some Practical Guidelines for Supervisors 24

The Challenge of Supervision in the Future 28

Dedication
for
My Three Sons

Howie: Who wants so much to make a sad planet laugh and laugh and laugh!

Wayne: Who "hears a different drummer" and dreams the magical dreams perhaps all people ought to dream!

Danny: Who delights at trying to be "all things to all men" . . . and may very well make it!

With eternal affection,
W.G.

Will Real Evaluation Please Stand Up

Administrators and supervisors in public schools across the land are charged (some would say burdened) with evaluating personnel, ranging from cafeteria and custodial employees to the central figures in the education process — teachers. In the past 20 years or so administrators have been beguiled by philosophies of "management." Many of our schools have evolved into facsimiles of factories as the MBO-cost effectiveness-accountability metaphors of management have become implanted in the thinking of those responsible for personnel evaluation. To compare the results of teaching with the results of manufacturing is both unfortunate and erroneous. Nonetheless, administrators and supervisors have become obsessed with the need to evaluate school personnel as demands for "productivity" in the public sector have increased. And it is no secret that administrators have responded to these public demands in almost reflex fashion.

Evaluating the teaching performance of someone else is serious business. Those who undertake it must understand full well that students come to school primarily to be taught, not to be "managed" (notwithstanding the need for "discipline," which, in a sense, is management incarnate). It may be commendable to make schools more responsive to the harsh realities of late 20th-century America, but the promissory rhetoric of management always exceeds its capacity to deliver — especially when trying to deal with the slippery matters of teaching and learning. In short, the logic and lexicon of the accountant with his relentless fixation on "the bottom line" is wholly inappropriate to the sensitivities, and sometimes mysteries, of how and why children learn or fail to learn.

The key to effective supervision and evaluation rests in making certain distinctions between the act of supervision and the subsequent act of evaluation — distinctions all too frequently overlooked by those charged with supervisory responsibilities. *Supervision and evaluation are not complicated.* This fastback is devoted to keeping simple things simple, and not needlessly entangling educational leaders in a labyrinth of dotted lines, flowcharts, arrows, and schematics so cherished by management models. Essentially, this fastback will:

- do away with some persistent fictions about evaluation;

- offer criteria for judging teachers' performance;

- discuss how and for whom to use either checklists or narrative reports of performance; and

- present guidelines for managing supervision, conducting classroom visits and supervisory conferences, and writing narrative reports.

Of Managerial Myths and Fairy Tales

In the words of Kojak, the super-macho detective of television fame, "Fairy tales, baby, I love 'em." In a more discreet way, that is exactly what many administrators and teachers have said to the professional types who vend advice about evaluating teachers and other employees in the public schools. To begin, let us do away with some persistent fictions.

FICTION: All evaluation must be "objective."

Educators have long been enamored with the spirit of scientism and its canons of objectivity. Written evaluation of someone's services is supposed to pulsate with that antiseptic quality called "objectivity." There is utterly *no objectivity* in evaluating someone else's performance. Someone assigned to judge the value of the services of someone else comes *value-loaded* to that activity. Judgments made on someone else's performance are highly personal and, very frankly, ought to be. The fact is that no matter how one looks at a problem, a personal point of view is probably the most powerful ingredient for assessing the quality of someone else's services. Even our courts have ruled that a supervisor's judgment can be supported as long as the technical competence and fairness of that supervisor have been established.

FICTION: Proper evaluation demands "data."

A persistent hoax afflicting evaluation of personnel in the public schools is the idea that "data gathering" — a kissin' cousin to scientism — is the best way for determining the quality of teachers in the classroom. And so we find a host of forms and devices for recording occurrences of teacher and student behavior that can then be logged and graphed with lofty objectivity. Such tallyings of data are better reserved for machines than they are for the human beings whose central business is supposed to be determining what and how students are learning. Managerial types have simply made the issue of observing someone else's work far more complicated than it really is. Under the guise of being scientific and objective, the collection of these kinds of data really thwarts what might otherwise be a constructive communication between two people discussing just how good the one's performance actually is. I am not saying here that "fencing off," or limiting the skills or behavior that are to be judged, is bad; it is not. I am saying that to attempt to reduce observation of human behavior to the sterility of objective "data gathering," in situations fraught with emotion and ego-defensiveness is sheer managerial folly. It only reduces what might have been a fruitful discourse to one of frustration and resentment.

FICTION: Only by direct observation can supervisors evaluate performance.

Another persistent fantasy under which some evaluators labor is the idea that observation in the classroom is the only bona fide way of assessing the work of a teacher. To be sure, classroom observation is still probably the most direct method an evaluator has for gathering impressions about teaching. However, there are many subtle and not-so-subtle sources of evaluative information that skilled observers use. Telephone calls, letters, and even conversations at the family dinner table about teacher behavior, both positive and negative, have a way of filtering through to administrators and supervisors who are in close touch with their communities.

For administrators to conduct all their supervision through classroom observation is more to intimidate than to evaluate. My guideline is: use classroom observations that yield the kind of information that is genuinely useful in improving the quality of instruction.

FICTION: Annual evaluations of all staff are necessary for a comprehensive supervisory program.

Many school districts have a standing policy that all certificated staff should be evaluated annually. An annual evaluation policy is yet another fiction that unnecessarily burdens a school system's supervisory staff. Some staff do not need to be evaluated annually; others need to be evaluated with far greater frequency. For example, many school districts have policies requiring nontenured teachers to be evaluated two, three, or more times a year. But factors other than the tenure issue should determine the periodicity of formal written evaluations. When earlier performance foreshadows continued excellence, annual evaluation becomes a ritualistic, time-consuming exercise.

How teachers and other employees in the school ought to be evaluated is a rather simple process. In essence, evaluation is: observing the performance of a teacher in the classroom, focusing those observations on certain accepted elements of sound performance, and rendering a judgment on the relative quality of that performance based on that day.

FICTION: A standard evaluation form should be used to insure consistency.

We have to fill out forms for nearly every one of life's activities, ranging from opening checking accounts to filing income taxes to registering dogs. Schools are no exception; their plethora of reporting systems relentlessly dissipates our professional energies. In the area of supervision, a fixation on form can sabotage substance. A supervisory form that is a checklist of primarily mechanical items such as bulletin boards, seating arrangements, room temperature, and the like is not likely to be much help in assessing the quality of instruction. Although such mechanical aspects of the teaching environment are worthy of comment, they do not get at the substance of good teaching. Even negotiated contracts that dictate the form of supervisory reports should not deter administrators from determining the style in which substance is presented — a style that uses language with clarity and precision.

Seeing What Should Be Seen: Quality in the Classroom

Recently, when asked the question: Are the proposed tax cuts fairly distributed? the noted economist Milton Friedman responded, "Fairness is in the eye of the beholder, not an objective characteristic." He is correct! Whether evaluating a teacher's performance in the classroom or an administrator's work methods or a secretary's productivity, every supervisor first needs to understand that being fair is not necessarily being neutral. Next a supervisor must understand the distinction between supervision (observing performance with a view toward improving it) and evaluation (judging performance based on accepted criteria of good teaching). As one cannot understand or appreciate a literary classic unless trained to know what to look for, so a supervisor cannot be effective without knowing the elements of good teaching. In short, an observer in a classroom, like a literary or a music critic, must have a repertoire of information and background on which to base judgments.

Below are criteria for judging performance that I believe are central to supervision and evaluation.

1. How well does the teacher deal with skills and concepts?

Supervision that ignores these two main ingredients of teaching is worthless. Skills and concepts can be taught both inductively (particular to general) and deductively (general to particular), and there are appropriate moments for each. Supervisors should help teachers decide which method is appropriate for the skill or concept involved. Unless a supervisor can distinguish between the teaching of a skill and a concept, unless the supervisor understands how to lead students from learning concepts to making inferences and syntheses, the writing of supervisory prose to "improve instruction" is sheer folly and a hoax. Incessant commentary about neat bulletin boards simply won't help teachers prepare students for the academic rigor needed to compete in today's world.

2. What is the level of scholarship in the classroom demonstrated by the teacher and expected of the students?

Whatever American teenagers may be (and most are delightful young people), they are generally not scholars! One of the chief missions of supervisors ought to be insistence on sound scholarship and the pursuit of scholarly aims. This is a tall order, given the anti-intellectual ambiance of the general culture, which the schools of this country inevitably mirror. Sound scholarship means teaching content that is significant, not trivial. Distinguishing content that is important and must be taught from that which is merely "interesting" or "nice to know" is what separates the master teacher from the amateur. Given the limited time for instruction, how a teacher plans the use of time with content of intellectual substance should be considered a prime criterion of performance.

3. How well does the teacher speak and write English?

In an era when the English language is misused and abused not only by teachers but by highly-paid radio and TV commentators, it is time to bring the speaking and writing of correct English back into vogue.

Teachers should be evaluated, at least in part, by how well they speak and write their native language. Their language habits should serve as a model to young people, many of whom have few acceptable models to emulate.

Nothing is as embarrassing to the image of public schools as to have their professional employees speak or write poorly or both (and this includes a supervisor who writes ungrammatical, inarticulate English in an evaluation report — a common phenomenon!). Incorrect spelling and grammatical errors in notes sent home, in comments on student papers, or, of all places, in writing on the blackboard, cannot be tolerated, especially in an era when so-called "basic skills" are very nearly apotheosized.

4. Does the teacher use a variety of teaching methods?

Varied methods of presenting information, of teaching skills, or of helping students to understand difficult concepts are included in the repertoires of outstanding teachers. However, choice of methods depends on the purpose of the lesson and the level of the students. A lecture is an appropriate method for quickly transmitting large volumes of factual information to groups but is hardly suitable for students in the primary grades or as an exclusive method for any age group. Judicious use of discussion, hands-on techniques for so-called "discovery" learning, Socratic questioning, and the like are all evidence of a teacher's technical competency and deserve attention and commentary in a supervisor's written evaluation.

5. Does the teacher maintain an appropriate level of control?

Concern over the quality of control (discipline) in a classroom could be called America's pathology — and with good reason. For the past decade discipline has been the number-one problem mentioned by respondents to the Gallup polls of public attitudes toward education. The problem of discipline is beyond the scope of this fastback, but many of the factors contributing to good discipline are subsumed under other criteria of good teaching discussed in this chapter. Good supervision need not dwell on this aspect of teaching unless the climate in the classroom is poor and control is inadequate. Control, like power, becomes an issue only when it is absent!

6. Does the teaching show evidence of good planning?

Planning and preparation of lessons is, of course, a supervisor's favorite, as it should be, for the less-than-adequate teacher. However, many fine teachers do not appear to do much planning, but with conspicuous regularity their teaching excites, stimulates, and generates serious inquiry in the classroom. Many first-rate teachers plan loosely but execute that planning superbly because of long experience with the subject matter and their knowledge of students.

Nothing stated here should be construed as "anti-planning"; but experienced teachers and supervisors know full well that lesson plans, however well drafted, are seldom fully executed, especially when the students become sufficiently intrigued with the subject that they engage in far more discussion than anyone might have anticipated.

In evaluating planning, the supervisor must keep perspective and balance orthodox regulation and expectation against dramatic, visible results, however unorthodox the means used to obtain them. Given the limited time for instruction, how a teacher plans for the use of time with material of intellectual substance should be considered a central criterion of performance.

7. Does the teacher demonstrate good pedagogical principles?

We know that inductive teaching, when done well, helps students to master material. Inductive teaching takes time, because it is a process of presenting detail, relating one detail to another, organizing the details into a logical sequence, and finally leading students to an intellectually defensible synthesis. Students are then able to synthesize from details presented; they are able to link cause and effect, thus leading them to find similar relationships in other situations. This is one superb result of inductive teaching.

Sound pedagogy should also be evident in the structure of a lesson. Essential ingredients of a well-developed lesson include the following:

— a clear introduction to establish purpose and direction

— development of skills needed to understand concepts

— periodic summaries and the use of searching questions to ascertain if students comprehend the material

— directed discussion to evoke generalizations and inferences

— review and evaluation to assure mastery of content

— assignments for further investigation

Although every lesson may not include all these ingredients (indeed, the master teacher might find them confining), they do provide the supervisor with some bench marks for evaluating classroom performance.

Another aspect of good pedagogy is the effective use of questions and anecdotes — prime ingredients of great teaching. Over many years, I have read hundreds of evaluation reports that are descriptive but seldom include any analytical commentary on the kinds and quality of questions asked. Yet we know that as a teacher Socrates and his contemporary disciples will never really be out of intellectual fashion. In addition to good questioning techniques, anecdotes and illustrations are also powerful teaching tools. Colorful stories, illustrative incidents, and interesting sidelights can illuminate generalities and help students to remember a concept they might otherwise have forgotten.

For example, Évariste Galois, the 19th century mathematician considered by many to be the father of modern mathematics, was killed in a duel at the age of 20. He had worked feverishly the preceding night to complete his central theoretical work in mathematics. Students do not need to know this story, but it may pique their interest and add some spice to the abstract study of mathematics. Similarly, the story of Antonio Salieri's intrigues against Mozart (the plot of the popular play, *Amadeus*) helps students to understand that this musical genius faced common human problems such as the petty vengeance and rivalry of his less talented peers. With the proper use of illustrative material of all kinds, teachers can ignite curiosity.

8. Do the results of achievement testing indicate continuing student growth?

Many teachers and the organizations representing them, and even many school administrators, resist the idea of using the result of achievement testing as one criterion for evaluating performance. This is unfortunate because such a defensive attitude bolsters the argument of critics who claim that the public schools are inadequate and that teachers refuse, behind their tenured ramparts, to compete on issues of quality in the "real" world — the way everybody else must.

Achievement testing (to be clearly distinguished from IQ or aptitude testing such as S.A.T.'s — the resident vampire of the American high school) provides an appropriate data base for assessing the outcomes of instruction. To the argument so frequently heard, "You mean you want me to teach for the test?" my response as a supervisor is, "I certainly do; if you have taught well what you deem a child must know, for what else would you teach? Isn't a test designed to determine if a child has mastered what you have taught?" Rearguard tactics designed to avoid the central issue of measuring clearly what a child is expected to know after a reasonable period of exposure to certain content are no longer acceptable. Besides, if a student's reading score rises by a full grade after only six months of teaching, and such results are almost uniform throughout the class, how does one not attribute this to superior teaching — especially if next door a class of similar abilities does not achieve similar results?

9. Does the teacher display a cooperative attitude in working with students and fellow staff?

We have made much of "relating with others" — too much, in my judgment. Popularity has all too frequently been confused with cooperativeness, and there ought to be a distinction. It does not necessarily follow that a "popular" teacher is a good one. An instructor who gives mostly A's to his students may be popular but is hardly professional. Faculty "loners" may be outstanding teachers; one does not need to party with the crowd every Friday to be a sound scholar! On the other hand, hostility, obstructionism, chronically contrary behavior, and general lack of cooperation need corrective action; their presence does, indeed, make for poor performance.

10. Does the teacher handle reports and procedural matters expeditiously?

Procedural fidelity cannot be ignored as a criterion for evaluating a teacher's work. Schools today are unavoidably entangled with procedures — forms to complete, data to report, regulations to enforce, orders to fill, bills to pay, calls to make. The failure of teachers to carry their share of this admittedly oppressive load is simply poor performance. Chronic lateness, failure to return corrected papers on time, excessive absences, failure to return parental phone calls, incomplete report cards — all are indicators of slipshod, low-quality performance and need to be corrected — quickly. Administrative silence despite repeated incidents of this kind is administrative negligence. In this regard, "Mr. Nice Guy" really is "Mr. Incompetent".

11. Is the teacher engaged in some program of professional growth?

Professional growth is a cliché in educational writing, a phrase that is tired and worn. Teachers also may be tired and worn. They need stimulation to continue their intellectual growth and they need to enhance their skills simply to stay in place. Feeble inservice courses and vacant workshops dealing with fashionable, narcissistic, self-indulging material (e.g., the "burnout" kick) will never help students to learn more or help teachers to become more skilled in their art.

One of the key functions of supervision is to suggest and even to direct ways and means of on-the-job improvement of academic background and professional skills.

One could list many other areas of the teaching universe as a focus for supervision, but the 11 discussed in this chapter were selected because they deal with what to look for in good teaching. The next chapter will deal with ways of reporting evaluations. Again, the emphasis is on keeping things simple.

Checklists vs. Narratives: Which to Use, How, and When

Educators like to talk about "individualizing" instruction. This precept is also applicable when supervising and evaluating teacher performance. Teachers are not alike in their intelligence, commitments, styles, and skills. Given these individual differences, an evaluation form that merely requires the supervisor to check off an adjective ("excellent," "good," etc.) or a number ("5," "4," "3," etc.) as a way of rating performance is hardly an adequate assessment instrument. Nevertheless, checklists do have some value. Let us consider first the merits of checklists and for whom they have the greatest utility.

Uses of Checklists

The problems beginning teachers typically face are usually related to classroom management and organization — poor control in the classroom, lack of careful planning, talking over the heads of pupils, insensitivity to matters of pacing instruction. With experience many beginning teachers overcome these problems on their own. But when these problems can be spotted early in the year on a checklist, an alert supervisor can salvage many potentially good teachers by showing them ways of correcting their deficiencies. The first year of teaching is difficult at best. Good supervision can ease the way.

With tenured teachers (and there are both good and bad ones), the checklist provides the supervisor with a means of pinpointing problems, particularly mechanical ones. And in follow-up conferences with teachers it provides a relatively objective record to use for making them aware of a problem and its severity and for logging recommendations for the elimination or amelioration of the problem.

Checklists help to keep the supervisor and the person being evaluated on target during the limited time available for a supervisory conference. A comprehensive checklist keeps a supervisor from dwelling on his/her special prejudices or philosophy of education, which may or may not be relevant to a teacher's immediate needs.

Given the excessive supervisory load of most administrators and the limited time in which to do evaluations, a checklist provides a format that is easy to complete in a short period of time. However, the virtue of efficiency is negated if the checklist is so full of ambiguities and vagueness of language that it is of little use as an evaluation instrument.

One could generate other arguments on behalf of checklists, but I believe that the preceding ones are the most important. Opponents of checklists on the other hand, consider them "instant" evaluation and offer counter-arguments of considerable weight.

Abuses of Checklists

A checklist can never be a truly accurate assessment of performance. For example, a rating scale simply manipulates the symbol system without adding one iota of descriptive data that might more accurately assess performance. One need only witness the indecisiveness of many administrators, who place the required "X" on the line between two categories on a scale, as illustrated below, to see the human factor that unavoidably lingers in judging the performance of a colleague.

Excellent	Good	Average	Needs Improvement
X			

Furthermore, such rating scales commonly used in checklists foster a report card, "wadjaget" mentality among teachers.

Checklists are too skeletal, too one-dimensional to be adequate evaluation devices. They can provide only limited measures of performance, particularly for experienced teachers.

Checklists act as tourniquets to the expansion of evaluative commentary. People are forced to write just enough to fill the space available (which is precious little on most checklists). Evaluative prose expands in direct proportion to the space available for commentary!

Checklists tend to induce greater evaluative generosity and charity than is sometimes warranted because they force the evaluator to make quick judgments; and in order to avoid conflict at a later time, the evaluator leans toward a positive rating. If evaluators place avoidance of conflict above accuracy of reportage, distortion occurs.

Keeping in mind the above discussion of the pros and cons of checklists, let us now turn to written narrative evaluations.

Narrative Evaluation Reports

Narrative evaluations have a good deal to commend them if the evaluator knows what to look for, can synthesize and make inferences from what is observed, and can write with clarity and precision. Essentially a narrative evaluation report should have three components:

1. Commentary by the evaluator on a limited number of substantial objectives to which each party had agreed earlier is the first component. Remarks on the extent to which a teacher accomplishes each objective are essential in this section, else the whole idea of writing such objectives becomes, in the minds of the faculty, no more than an administrative fetish.

2. Description of the quality of performance rendered in a specified period is the second ingredient of a narrative evaluation. This section, however must be preceded by analysis of a teacher's accomplishment of objectives if it is to be used to induce growth and improvement. It is in this descriptive section that the indicators of high quality teaching become the focus for detailed and analytical assessment and commentary and establish the groundwork for the final component of the narrative evaluation.

3. Recommendations for precise ways to improve performance cap

the narrative evaluation. No evaluation can be considered complete without *prescription* following *description.* In fact, a number of court cases have clearly established that help in the form of precise suggestions is a minimum essential of sound evaluative practice; and this responsibility falls squarely on administrators and supervisors.

Narratives should neither gush unearned praise nor bristle with electric harshness; they should laud what is truly commendable — not applaud mere routine. Negative criticism should be bridled and balanced: phrased delicately for those who are inexperienced but cooperative and willing; stiffened with candor for those who refuse to respond to more gentle prodding. To avoid the trap of being either too generous or too critical when using checklists with adjectival ratings ("excellent", "good", etc.), supervisors should be able to justify in precise language what these ratings mean on an item-by-item basis. Such justifications should state briefly and crisply the reasons for the rating and include illustrations. To be sure, this involves extra time, but it adds to the integrity of the process.

Negative remarks are most defensible legally when they follow the pattern of 1) comment, 2) illustration and 3) suggestion. If a teacher has a problem with discipline, it should be precisely stated, illustrated by an incident or incidents actually observed, and then followed by specific suggestions for eliminating or reducing the problem.

To conclude, a checklist, well-conceived and executed, is generally useful for younger, inexperienced faculty; but a narrative is a far more useful and sophisticated evaluation instrument for teachers with senior status. Common sense, logic, and simplicity are far more critical in sound evaluative systems then dizzying managerial lexicons and diagrammed shell games.

Some Practical Guidelines for Supervisors

Continuing with an emphasis on keeping things simple, in this chapter, I shall present some practical guidelines for managing supervision, for conducting classroom observations, and for writing narrative evaluations.

On Supervisory Systems

1. Establish different ways and calendars for evaluating nontenured and tenured teachers; they are different breeds — at least for the usual two or three probationary years — and should be treated differently. Given these differences, there should be flexibility in the time of year, frequency of observation, length of conferences, kinds of objectives to be emphasized, and forms on which assessments are rendered.

2. Classroom visits by supervisors should always be *unannounced!* A staged performance is not what a supervisor comes to observe. Teachers are paid for teaching well *all the time,* and they should be willing to navigate the rigors of surprise scrutiny.

3. Supervisory time is better served when full period observations are not required. They frequently serve no useful purpose other than meeting procedural requirements. Often it is more useful to do three 20-minute observations in one week, the first at the beginning of a period, the second during the middle, and the last during the closing of a lesson. This allows the observer to see the sequence of a program, which a single period observation does not.

4. Scheduled observations should never block on-the-spot written evaluations when needed. Nor should negotiated contracts be permitted to limit the scope of evaluative work. Some situations need immediate action and call for a "memorandum of concern," which registers dissatisfaction about a serious problem. Such a communication allows the supervisor to deal quickly with teachers who are performing poorly and serves as record of supervisory concern for use in potential court suits having to do with violations of personnel procedures in dismissal cases.

5. Encourage self-evaluation in the supervisory process. Asking a teacher to state how well he/she thought a lesson went or how productive the year was helps to set the stage for fruitful exchanges. A good practice is to design a form for written self-assessments, which can be attached to the supervisor's written comments.

6. Don't encumber evaluation policy with unnecessary regulations or requirements, such as a specific number of visits in classrooms. All too frequently, well-meaning but overzealous central administrations and boards of education place unreasonable quantitative demands for supervision on supervisory staff. The result is low quality documents that are poorly written, intellectually vacuous, and useless as instruments for ways of improving instruction. Such reports may fulfill all procedural demands but essentially they are file-stuffers — not much else. In short, keep requirements simple and sensible; results of a highly acceptable order may very well follow.

On Classroom Visits

1. Supervisors have frequently been taught not to take notes because teachers find it intimidating. Well, teachers may find the results of supervisors' faulty memories not only intimidating, but infuriating! Supervisors should always take notes during formal visits. Such notes should include exact quotes (from teachers or students) relating to issues the observer intends to describe or expand on in the written narrative; a good quote can illustrate well what might otherwise be a bland generality.

2. Supervisors should not interrupt the teacher during instruction. Except on rare occasions, they should not permit themselves to be drawn into the class deliberations — despite the polite attempts of some teachers to do just that in a kind of flattering deference to authority. Supervisors should leave and enter the room as unobtrusively as possible. Effusive greetings and lengthy exchanges between supervisor and teacher have no place in such situations; quiet "hellos" or appropriate nods of recognition are enough.

3. A report on a classroom visit should be written within 24 hours after that observation. A teacher is anxious enough without worrying about a pending report. The supervisor who delays completing evaluation reports can no more be excused than the teacher who makes a major assignment and then either fails to correct it or delays its return to students for so long that the purpose of the assignment has been effectively dissipated.

On Conducting Supervisory Conferences

1. A sound supervisory conference is what both parties make of it. Each should come prepared to discuss intelligently and dispassionately what happened in the classroom. Setting a time limit for the conference helps to keep things focused. Each party wants to get on with the task at hand; so get on with it!

2. A supervisor should begin by having the teacher react to the lesson — its content, methods used, and the general tone and conduct of the class. Follow this with directed discussion about the positive and negative aspects of the lesson, as perceived by both the supervisor and the teacher. Indicate areas where improvement should be made and ask what help or resources are needed. When the observation report is less than positive, the supervisor and teacher should agree on what the next steps should be.

3. A supervisor must be sensitive to the emotional context of the conference, the outcome of which may determine a teacher's professional future. Heated exchanges are nearly always counterproductive.

4. Supervisors should secure the teacher's signature on the written

observation report, but they should make the teacher aware that a signature merely indicates *receipt of the document* not agreement to or acquiescence in its substance. Also, teachers have every right to append appropriate coments to any material about to become part of their professional files — and the supervisor should tell them that at the conference.

On Writing Narratives

One need not be a literary stylist to write clear English prose. Writing well is a craft few have really mastered, but most people can go beyond merely "muddling through." Following are a few hints for writing clear and precise narrative evaluational reports:

1. Do not overwhelm teachers with polysyllabic jargon in the hope that it will impress them and others who may read the report. Use simple and direct language that communicates the first time you read it. Bear in mind that clarity and compression are central virtues in writing expository prose.

2. Think before you write. In describing and prescribing, try to create verbal photographs of what you see and what you advise.

3. Check your report for errors in spelling, punctuation, and grammar; such errors call into question the competence of the supervisor.

4. Proofread carefully! Once an evaluator has signed a document, there are no more "typos"; there are only mistakes!

The Challenge of Supervision in the Future

In recent years there has been considerable concern expressed in the media and by respected researchers and teacher educators about the quality of candidates entering the teaching profession. Obviously, the economy is a factor. Teaching is a depressed job market in most parts of the nation, and there are few indications that this situation will change in the next decade. Bright young people know this and they are choosing career options with more opportunities and better pay. And some of our most academically able teachers are leaving the field for the same reasons. Another piece of evidence is that in 1979-80, young people indicating teaching as a vocational choice were scoring 85 points below the national average on verbal S.A.T.'s and 48 points below the average in mathematics. Clearly, we may be fast approaching the time when a shortage of intellectual raw material will rule out the possibility for academic excellence in our schools.

If these negative indicators persist, then the role of supervision and evaluation becomes ever more important. The challenge is clear: to establish the conditions and climate for teachers' continued intellectual growth in order to insure that children and youth are taught properly that which they must know.

Some would make a pseudo-science out of supervision and evaluation. The guidelines I have discussed in the fastback are more humble. But we do have some tools and some common agreements that help us reach consensus on what is high quality teaching. That is about the best we can hope for in a process fraught with subjectivity, emotional tension, and sometimes prejudice. However flawed the process, it is still useful as long as we recognize that in judging human behavior the units of measurement remain eternally imperfect.